LIVING WREATHS

20 BEAUTIFUL PROJECTS FOR GIFTS AND DÉCOR

NATALIE BERNHISEL ROBINSON

Photographs by **SUSAN BARNSON HAYWARD**

GIBBS SMITH
TO ENRICH AND INSPIRE HUMANKIND

First Edition
18 17 16 15 14   5 4 3 2 1

Published by
Gibbs Smith
P.O. Box 667
Layton, Utah 84041

1.800.835.4993 orders
www.gibbs-smith.com

Designed by Michelle Thompson | Fold & Gather Design
Printed and bound in China
Gibbs Smith books are printed on either recycled, 100% post-consumer waste, FSC-certified
papers or on paper produced from sustainable PEFC-certified forest/controlled wood source.
Learn more at www.pefc.org.

Library of Congress Cataloging-in-Publication Data

Robinson, Natalie Bernhisel.
 Living wreaths : 20 beautiful projects for gifts and décor / Natalie Bernhisel Robinson ;
photographs by Susan Barnson Hayward. – First edition.
    pages cm
 ISBN 978-1-4236-3264-1
1. Wreaths. 2. Gardens, Miniature. I. Hayward, Susan Barnson. II. Title.
 SB449.5.W74B47 2014
 635–dc23
                        2013029031

For my husband, Matthew,
with love and boundless gratitude,
and for my two beautiful children, Felix and Olive—
you make life worth living.

Love, Inspire, Create.

CONTENTS

ACKNOWLEDGMENTS

This *Living Wreaths* book challenged me to my core and pushed me well outside my comfort zone. I spent many hours in the fetal position, in my closet, wondering if I could accomplish this goal. Pull off elaborate flower arrangements for a wedding—no problem, but write a book!? (Gasp!) I had to keep repeating, "I think I can, I think I can, I think I can," and guess what, I did it! I'm so honored to express my gratitude for those who have helped me along the way.

Thank you, Matt, my incredible husband and best friend for holding my hand through this exciting book-writing process. You became well accustomed to having living wreaths take over the house and the yard. There were living wreaths in the sink, wreaths on the floor, wreaths on the counter, wreaths in the driveway and moss everywhere!

Thank you to my darling children who were so patient with me while writing and photographing this book. I loved having you both with me during the long days photographing. As a five-year-old and two-year-old, you became living wreath experts yourselves, helping me pick out beautiful succulents and collecting clumps of moss for wreaths while playing in the backyard.

I called upon family and friends for inspiration and your ideas and words were so helpful. A special thanks to my amazing father and mother, Kurt and Betsy Bernhisel, and to my four beautiful sisters—Heather, Ashlie, Allison and Sarahjane. A special thank-you to my dear friends, Erika Sheffield-Stull and Alison Gates.

I was lucky enough to work with the most creative and talented friend and photographer Susan Hayward. You truly captured the stunning and simplistic beauty of my wreaths. Thank you!

A big thank-you to my amazing editor, Hollie Keith, for first coming to me with this project and for always extending my deadlines just a little further. Your insights and hard work are much appreciated.

"The only difference between an extraordinary life and an ordinary one is the extraordinary pleasures you find in ordinary things."

–Veronique Vienne

The wreath is a symbol of life, eternity, welcome and comfort. A ring to hang on your front door that calls, "Come inside, old friend." Wreaths are frequently the most impressive of displays, whether draped over a fireplace or hung as a grand welcome on a front door. From the simplest herb wreath to the more extravagant succulent design, their strong outlines and shapes have great visual impact. Whatever the time of year, a wreath adds a cheerful breath of fresh air to surroundings.

I've always had a love of flowers and floral designing from an early age. I would find myself gathering flowers, grasses, branches and leaves from my mother's backyard. My favorites have always been the fuzzy pussy willows and blooming branches that make a joyful appearance in early spring. The first signs of those glorious blooms and buds make my heart sing and tell me that I can hold on just a little bit longer, warmer weather is on the way. I started taking some of my clippings and decided it would be easy enough to wire them onto a wreath form. It IS easy! This then progressed into a full-fledged

wreath-making business, and into my current floral company, La Fleur. I've never given up the love of finding natural materials in my own backyard or in the beautiful mountains of Utah. I certainly always have garden snips in my car in hopes I see some lovely red dogwood branches, berried juniper or fragrant sagebrush (my new obsession). I call this snipping in the wild "harvesting," and I've been known to do it under the cover of darkness. You bet I know where I can find lily of the valley blooming behind the local bank or where all the ginkgo trees are in the city so I can find some leaves for a bridal bouquet. I know it may be tempting to go clip bundles of blooming forsythia in your neighbor's yard at midnight, but I assure you, it's easier to just knock on the door and ask.

There is nothing like plunging your nose into the deeply intense fragrance of bay leaf, eucalyptus and evergreens. Sniff deep. The scent of bay leaf takes my mind to the beginning of December and the holiday season when I start decorating the house. Fresh bundles of bay decorate the mantelpiece and tabletops, bringing the outdoors in, to create a botanical wonderland. Hand-wired wreaths of evergreens and pinecones fill each window and door front. Wreath making releases a glorious fresh scent as you work and creates a magnificent decoration. I find great pleasure in adorning my home with such fragrance and beauty, and find it a warm and welcoming way to greet gatherings of family and friends during the coldest winter months.

December also brings about my annual wreath-making classes. It started out with only a few students and quickly grew. I find that most people are delighted in taking nature's bounty and making creations that decorate our homes and surroundings, and to possibly gift to friends and family. The appeal of using natural materials is that you are immediately bestowed with an exquisite color scheme that is at one with the surroundings. By working with the seasons, you are continually being presented with new materials that provide an ever-revolving cycle of different textures and forms. Nature is the best designer. The subtlety of natural colors and the variety of forms can never quite be matched by anything we could ever dream up. I love teaching a new skill to willing students. They come to class shy and intimidated, thinking they may not be "crafty" enough. Students end up leaving with beautiful, fresh, handmade wreaths. Heads are held high with the look of achievement on their faces. They have created something unique and wondrous with their own hands, and I'm so proud to be their teacher.

Most crafters and do-it-yourselfers focus on the temporary wreath. After the season, you are left with dried leaves and crispy crumbling boughs. I find myself bowing my head and having a moment of silence with my beautiful creation as I toss it into the garbage bin. Single tear. But dry your eyes, friends, because this book is about the living wreath. It does as the name implies—it lives on! Simply water regularly and watch them grow! With the newfound skills this book will teach, you can make living wreaths for any season. Imagine how fun it will be to have family and friends gather materials and have a creative wreath-making party.

When you begin making your own wreaths, you will be amazed to discover yet another design style—your own. Use this book as a guide, but undoubtedly make some subtle changes, add different plant varieties, different colors, textures, etc. Enjoy your personalized interpretation of the wreath designs and be assured that it's difficult to make an incorrect wreath. It's not wrong; embrace the non-perfection and wildness of your creation. If you do not love the results, simply add a few plants and just remove elements and give something new a whirl. Many different plants, succulents and cactuses adapt nicely in the basic living wreath style. More than just a wreath, it is a garden in miniature, one that changes continuously. It will be fun and exciting for you to make your wreath discoveries.

Happy harvesting and wreath making!

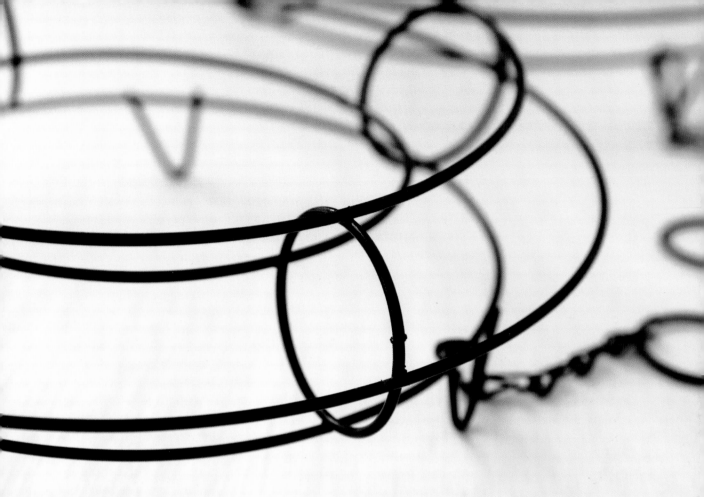

MATERIALS AND USEFUL TOOLS

This is what you will need to starting creating a living wreath.

- Plastic sheeting or a large garbage bag to cover your work surface
- Latex gloves
- Wire wreath frame
- Potting soil
- Water-retaining crystals
- Sheet moss

- Spool of 20- to 22-gauge copper wire
- Wire cutters
- Garden shears
- Screwdriver, chopstick or wooden skewer
- Forceps
- U-shaped wire or pins
- Plant and flower varieties

PLASTIC SHEETING

Use plastic sheeting or a large garbage bag to cover your work surface. This will protect your worktable and allow easy clean up.

LATEX GLOVES

Latex gloves will protect your hands while wrapping the wire frame with moss. Moss can irritate the skin, so this is a good precaution. The latex is thin and allows you to plant and create your living wreath quite easily, opposed to bulky gardening gloves. I do, however, suggest wearing heavy gloves when making the cactus wreath.

WIRE FRAMES

Every living wreath owes its beginning to a wire frame or base. The hollow structure will hold soil, moss and plant matter. You can purchase wire frames designed specifically for construction of living wreaths, and most come with a hanging chain. The frames used on this book were purchased from TopiaryArtworks.com. If you are going to take the time to make a living wreath, why not purchase quality materials that insure a long-lasting creation? Wreath frames come in an array of fun shapes and sizes, such as a classic round shape and, for a more modern design, square and rectangular shapes. Consequently, the importance of choosing the right base can't be underestimated.

SOIL

For succulent and cactus living wreaths, I like using a soil made specifically for these low-water varieties. Other wreaths will benefit from a standard potting soil with an added fertilizer. If a living wreath is to sustain flowers, fruit and lush green foliage, the demands for nutrients and water will exceed that of a succulent wreath. Polymer water-retaining crystals are capable of holding approximately 200 times their weight in water, and they are ideal for moisture-loving plants. Polymers are inexpensive and can be found in the garden section of your local garden store. Follow the manufacturer's recommended amounts on the package, and add them to the quantity of soil suggested below.

The water-retaining polymers are mixed into the moist soil an hour before planting to allow full absorption of the water. As the crystals absorb the water and swell, they increase the bulk of the soil. Without the water-retaining crystals, your wreath will dry out rather quickly, especially in the heat of summer months.

SOIL QUANTITIES

10-inch wreath–¾ gallon

12-inch wreath–1 gallon

14-inch wreath–1 ½ gallons

18-inch wreath–2 ½ gallons

MOSS

Sheet moss, or sphagnum moss, is the best type of moss to use in a living wreath application. Sphagnum moss is the kind most commonly used to build moss-lined hanging baskets. It is sold by the bag or by the pound. It can be difficult to gauge the exact amount needed since it does not have a uniform density. Because of that, it's wise to have a surplus supply for patching thin areas and tucking around plants.

MOSS QUANTITIES

10-inch wreath—1 pound

12-inch wreath—1–2 pounds

14-inch wreath—2 pounds

18-inch wreath—3–4 pounds

WIRE

Twenty- or 22-gauge copper wire is an excellent choice for the construction of a wreath. It's heavy duty and will not corrode. If you can't find copper wire on a spool, wrap loosely coiled wire onto your own paddle or empty spool.

WIRE WRAPPING

10-inch wreath–40 inches of wire

12-inch wreath–50 inches of wire

14-inch wreath–60 inches of wire

18-inch wreath–80 inches of wire

FISHING LINE

For the living moss wreath, it's best to secure the moss on top of the wreath form with fishing line.

WIRE CUTTERS

Don't dull your garden shears or scissors by cutting wire. Pick up a pair of wire cutters at the hardware store.

GARDEN SHEARS

A strong pair of spring-loaded shears will cope with most material. Always use a pair that feels comfortable to work with.

SCREWDRIVER OR WOODEN SKEWER

You'll need some sort of sharp tool to poke holes in the finished living wreath base. This will allow for space to place roots and plants. A screwdriver works great or even a wooden skewer, chopstick or pencil.

FORCEPS

I really can't imagine planting a living wreath without this useful tool. Not only can the forceps make the planting holes, but it also holds delicate stems and allows for roots to be tucked into the soil easily. Forceps are a must-have while handling prickly cactuses.

U-SHAPED WIRE OR PINS

U-shaped pins or small 2-inch pieces of wire bent into a U shape will help secure cuttings and plants while roots take hold.

PLANTS

Most plants that work well in a container garden will work within a living wreath application. Chapters will identify specific plant choices and designs, and how best to get started.

1 THE WORK AREA

Select a work area out of direct sun but with good lighting. Inside is fine too. You will need plenty of space in which to work if you are to keep organized. First, make sure that your work surface is at the right height. Waist-high level will be the most comfortable and efficient, anything lower will have you hunched over with a strained back. If your table is not waist level, trying using some bricks or cement blocks to elevate it to the correct height. Wreaths are best made if you remain standing, especially as you should often move back to assess progress, and you will probably need to be on your feet to select materials and supplies.

2 PLASTIC SHEETING

Spread plastic sheeting or an unused large garbage bag to cover the work surface before beginning. The plastic will allow you to easily turn the wreath base during construction and planting. Place any tools you will need to the side of the work area, within easy reach.

3 MOSS PREPARATION

Ready the moss and remember to slip on latex gloves. Give the moss a good soak before starting wreath construction. Fill a bucket with cool water and submerge the moss and allow it to really absorb the water. Ring it out well, and remember to save this nutrient-rich mossy water for watering your garden. You will want to begin making your wreath with damp moss.

4 FORM THE MOSS MAT

Place your well-drained damp moss into the middle of the work surface. Sheet moss has a more attractive green top and a lower rooted area. Turn the green side facing down and the rooted area facing up, since it will be reversed during wrapping. Make a circular shape with the moss, approximately two and half times the diameter of the wire frame. You will have a much easier time if using a generous amount of moss. Lay down the frame to make sure there is enough moss to wrap all the way around. Try to keep large sections of the moss intact, and open pieces that have been doubled over in packing. Large, flat sections of moss work best, with a thickness of approximately 1½ inches deep. Add extra moss to thin areas to prevent soil from leaking through. It's a good idea to have a large pile of patch moss ready for the wire-wrapping process.

5 PLACING THE WREATH FRAME

Lay the wire wreath frame onto the prepared moss mat. Some of the tubular wire forms have little wedge feet on one side, which allow for the wreath to be elevated somewhat while hanging or laying on a tabletop. Make sure the feet are facing down while you wrap the wreath. Take off the hanging clip and set it aside. You can reattach it onto the wreath once it is completed. You can leave it attached, but it tends to get in the way and might get caught up inside the wreath as you are wrapping.

6 SOIL

Start placing the moist potting soil over the wire frame so that it fills the inside of the hollow wire structure. Gently pat the soil but do not over compress and compact it. Roots like air spaces within the soil.

7 FOLDING MOSS OVER THE SOIL

View your wreath like a map with four directions. Lift moss from the outside north, then south, east and west points, laying it on the top of the soil core. This will make for an even wreath base.

8 WIRE WRAPPING

Open the spool of wire to a 6-inch length and place it underneath the moss mat with the frame and soil on top. While holding the moss with one hand, pass the spool of wire up over the top and back around. Lift the moss slightly so as not to disturb the soil and just high enough to pass the spool under it. Repeat this on the same section to overlap the wire. This will ensure your wire is very secure, and won't start unraveling as you continue wrapping. Twist the beginning of the wire together with the wire from the spool and pull it taut so that it disappears into the moss. Repeat passing the spooled wire underneath the wreath base. Wrap the wire every ¾ inch, or the width of your forefinger is a good measurement. You'll think to yourself, This is such a mess! I think I'm

doing something wrong! Somebody please help me! Don't panic. The moss will open up and soil will spill out, and it will look as if you've made a terrible mistake. You haven't, this is normal. Just keep scooping the soil back into the frame and use a lot of patch pieces of moss. Keep wrapping with the wire, and don't give up! You can do this! It will all come together in the end.

Maintain a taut tension on the copper wire as you repeatedly pass it beneath the base. If you happen to pull on your spool of wire with too much tension and it breaks, don't worry. Simply twist and secure the broken piece of wire, and start again with the spool of wire. The plastic sheeting underneath your wreath can be rotated during construction to maintain your most comfortable position.

Once the entire wreath is wired together, flip it over and look for any spots that might need some patching. Usually the underside has some visible soil, so just patch up those areas with more moss. Keep the wire attached and wrap it around, filling in any thin spots.

9 ENDING THE WRAPPING

When you come to the end of wrapping, join the beginning 6-inch tail wire with the wire on the spool. Cut off the wire and tuck any excess into the moss.

10 YOU ARE NOW READY TO STARTING PLANTING!

Whew, you did it! Go pour yourself a celebratory drink.

A few ideas about finished wreath bases–

Wreath bases can be made and kept indefinitely in a dry place. When you are ready to start planting, soak and drain the wreath and get started.

Wreath bases can be recycled into new living wreaths once blooming is finished. They can be replanted with new seedlings for a new look and purpose.

TIPS FOR HANGING

I love the ease of hanging a living wreath using the wire wreath frames that come with a chain and hook. They are strong, durable and ready to use. If you purchase wreath frames that do not have a provided hook, I suggest using strong picture-hanging wire. Attach it to the back of the wreath, directly onto the wire frame. If you've made your wreath base properly, you'll notice that it can be hard to find the wreath base frame inside all the wrapping of moss and soil. You'll have to stick your forceps or fingers inside and open up a section on the back of your wreath to thread your picture-hanging wire through. Tie securely using a double knot.

If you are creating a wreath of 18 inches or larger, then use two parallel hanging wires to disperse the load and prevent sagging. Always test the weight-bearing hook or nail on your door or wall before hanging.

When hanging a living wreath, you will want to allow for proper drainage first. A sopping-wet wreath can damage a painted door or wall. After thoroughly watering a wreath, place it on a raised surface that will allow for drainage and for air to circulate around it. Using upside-down terracotta pots as a stand for a draining wreath is a good option.

For a tabletop wreath, use a sturdy plastic dish that is made for a plant that would be placed on your floor. The dish is low enough that the wreath will get plenty of air circulation, and the moss peeking through disguises the clear plastic. The large hardware stores carry these in an array of sizes.

SUCCULENTS

The flamboyant succulent wreath celebrates the subtle color and echoes the dramatic circular shape of succulents. A welcome addition to any rustic wall, the succulents in the following wreaths simply generate sunshine. Succulent wreaths have an abundant fresh feel that will inject life into any environment.

SUCCULENT CUTTINGS

Multiple online resources such as Etsy and Amazon are available to purchase a wide variety of succulent cuttings. The grower selects an array of varieties and ships them directly to you, wrapped in paper and ready to plant. It's quite exciting opening this package to reveal such beautiful little jewels that will grow and flourish in your living wreath. You can also purchase succulent plants from garden centers to create your own cuttings. Allow new cut stems to callus over for two days prior to wreath construction. The callus end is the hard scab-like area the plant will root from. Succulents root easily when soil and moss are kept moist.

SUCCULENT PLANTS

Succulents with attached roots can also be easily planted into a living wreath. You can simply purchase a handful of plants and have a living wreath completed in hardly any time at all. Carefully remove most of the soil from the roots by scraping with your forceps, or even give the roots a dunk in fresh cool water to remove even more of the soil. Now get planting!

DESIGN AND PLANTING TECHNIQUES

WREATH DESIGN

First you will want to plan your wreath design. Succulent living wreaths are constructed in quite a straightforward way, but to achieve a flowing feel of unrestrained opulence requires careful positioning of materials. It is important to keep a good balance of color and shape, so stand back as often as possible and take a good look. There is no right or wrong way to go about planting the succulents into your wreath. Have courage, you can't mess this up! You can plant in a circular pattern along the outer ring and make your way around until you reach the center. The base will resemble a wreath upon a wreath. I prefer to fill and complete one section of the wreath at a time, starting on one side and completely planting until I reach all the way around.

For a pleasing and natural design, stagger the shapes and sizes as to not resemble a bull's-eye target. Mix and match different colors, textures, sizes and varieties or do a mass grouping of a solid color. I also find that clustering two large similar succulents on one side of the wreath, with one additional large succulent on the opposing side to balance the design and to create a stunning focal point works great. Another easy technique, especially for a beginner, is to create your design on your work surface before you start planting. Lay out your succulent cuttings on the table in a wreath shape, moving plants around until you end up with a pleasing design. After your design is laid out, you can start planting the succulents into your wreath.

1 Start with a damp living wreath base.

2 With forceps, a wooden skewer or a screwdriver, make a hole through the moss into the core of the wreath-base soil. Planting with forceps is ideal and highly recommended! Forceps allow for easy placement of slender, delicate stems into the soil. They can also open a wedge or hole in the wreath base, and the tips help tuck in delicate roots.

3 Insert the succulent cutting or the plant roots into the hole as deeply as possible. Push the surrounding moss and soil toward the stem from all directions to secure. Add a pinch of extra moss around the stem to fill in the hole, if needed.

4 If the succulent feels as if it might fall out, add a U-shaped pin for support. A 1½-inch wire bent into a U-shape is a great size. You can make larger pins to secure larger succulents. I tend to use quite a few pins in my succulent wreath making, especially around the steep outer sides of the base. You don't want all your hard work to come undone! Never stick the pin into the flesh of the stem or leaf, but, rather, position the pin to straddle the section. On a large succulent rosette that can be quite heavy, I've pinned around the stem from below and even gently straddled down on top of a leaf for added support. Be sure not to crush the plump leaves.

After planting, the wreath should lay flat for five to six weeks to help roots take hold.

WATERING

Succulents are easy to care for, as they don't need a lot of water to flourish. Most succulents are drought tolerant and are accustomed to long periods between watering. Squeeze the wreath from behind, if the base is hard and dry, give it a deep watering. If the moss is dry on the outside but soft inside when you squeeze, do not water. Water the wreath once every two weeks by fully submerging it in water for two to three minutes or until the bubbles that escape cease coming to the surface. If watering with a garden hose is preferred, take the utmost care. A heavy stream of water from your hose will knock all your beautifully rooted succulents loose. A slow dribble from the hose is an effective wreath-watering procedure, provided that it's done at a slow and gentle rate with repeated applications. Succulents do not tolerate overwatering or misting in particular along with most other plants in general. Make sure to drain thoroughly before you rehang.

HANGING LOCATION

Think about where you want to hang a succulent wreath. Succulents can look different and vary in color and texture depending on sun exposure. I suggest keeping your newly constructed wreath in bright light but out of direct sunlight for one week and then gradually introduce it to full exposure. However, wreaths might benefit most in partial shade from the midday sun. To be on the safe side, protect all succulent wreaths from freezing temperatures. Bright light is generally a requirement for the healthy growth of succulent wreaths, with protection from midday sun in intense heat. The same bright-light needs exist for indoor succulent wreaths.

ECHEVERIA

The simplicity of the sea-glass-blue echeveria is stunning. This variety is found at most garden centers, so putting together a living wreath will be a snap! I used 6 to 7 plants for a simple wreath design, with some of the moss base exposed. For an even more striking display, completely fill the wreath with solid echeveria. The large rosettes can be rather heavy, so make sure to secure the roots with U-shaped pins. For added support, you can pin down some of the under leaves using the straddle technique. Roots can also be cut off from the echeveria and allowed to callus over and root again while snuggly planted in the wreath base.

11-inch wreath base

MIXED
SUCCULENT 1

The various shapes, colors and textures of these succulents make
my heart go pitter-patter. I assure you planting succulent cuttings
will not be difficult, but it will take some time, so be patient and
have fun creating this unique piece of art.

9-inch wreath base
Approximately 100 cuttings

HENS AND CHICKS

Hens and chicks are one of my all-time favorite succulent varieties. I have them growing all over my yard and spilling out of numerous pots and containers. They are very happy grouped together and will spread nicely. The deep grey green rosettes with rosy red centers pop next to the bright green variety. Take some of the new-growth chicks and start a new wreath!

11-inch wreath base
9–10 (3-inch) succulents (with any extra chicks
growing off each mother plant)

MIXED
SUCCULENT 2

In this more modern-looking wreath, I grouped like succulents in thick sections around the circular form. The single large, ruffled pink-edged succulent makes for a beautiful focal point.

9-inch wreath base
10–12 (2-ich) succulents

SUCCULENT AND
FLOWER

The fleshy succulents in juxtaposition with the delicate blooms of alyssum make a beautiful pairing.

9-inch wreath base
25 succulent cuttings
12 flower seedling plugs

MIXED FLOWERS

This floral wreath suggests a nod to the past with petunias, impatiens and alyssum in shades of white and pinks. When choosing the flowers that will bloom in your wreath, keep in mind the wide variety of options. Flowers provide wonderful color and texture contrast to the stark beauty of a weathered barn door. Color, texture and shape can be a wonderful showcase in wreath form. There can be grand and small-scale designs to suite every occasion and situation.

Plant material that is very young, even before the flower color shows, is easier to plant and the most capable of making the adjustment to the living wreath base. Select healthy plants that are still in bud and that have loose roots. Mature specimens look tempting in the nursery, but they invite failure.

15-inch wreath base
40 seedling plugs in a mixture of varieties

PLANNING THE DESIGN

Pick an array of plants that will showcase charmingly open faces bursting with summertime color. I used a combination of white and pink petunias, impatiens and alyssum. My wreath can be used solely for inspiration. Choose whatever colors suit your mood or garden. Other flower varieties that work beautifully in living wreaths are pansy, lobelia, nasturtium and begonias.

Get started by first laying out your design on a work surface. Cluster petunias and impatiens together, and add in alyssum in equal areas around the wreath to give billowy softness. Once you have a good design planned, you can start planting.

PREPPING THE PLANTS

Gently remove plants from their plastic pots. Using forceps, scrape off excess soil to expose the roots.

PLANTING THE FLOWERS

1 The planting technique for a floral living wreath is near the same as planting a succulent wreath. Start by poking holes into the wreath form using forceps or a screwdriver.

2 Spacing plants every 3 to 5 inches, depending on the plant size, is not too close. Wreath plants are spaced much closer than if they were growing in a garden.

3 If the root ball is small enough, gently squeeze it to fit the slit in the base and ease in the roots with the forceps. Large older plants will be nearly impossible to plant into the wreath form. Try rinsing the soil off the root ball to reduce the size without damaging the roots. With forceps, ease the roots into the slit you have made in the wreath base.

4 Don't plant in the inner circle of your frame, or the round wreath shape will be lost. It's also helpful to note that a finished planted wreath is approximately 4 inches larger than the wire wreath base form.

5 This wreath should remain flat for two weeks before hanging.

CARE

Mixed flower living wreaths do best in sun or partial sun with evenly moist soil. Shade diminishes the bloom cycles, and in hot weather a weekly fertilizer application will keep the plants producing. Regular pruning and removing faded blooms will help maintain a healthy wreath.

Water the wreath by fully submerging in water once or twice a week for two to three minutes or with a long and gentle soak with a garden hose. If watering by hose, spray a stream of water over the wreath, wait a few minutes and then repeat the procedure to allow the wreath to become fully saturated. Drain well before rehanging.

CACTUS

I've always had a fondness for the desert. I'm drawn like a magnet to the orange and coral colors, the worn smooth sandstone, the heat, the textures, the flora and fauna. When I see a barrel cactus, prickly pear or blue agave, I think all is right in the world! We can all have a little piece of the desert right at home with a cactus living wreath.

Although wreaths are usually hung on a wall or door, they can be very effective as a table decoration. I imagine this thorny lovely on your table as you sip a frosty margarita! *Ole!* This wreath is not for the faint of heart; however, you will be richly rewarded with a daring conversation piece.

You'll need a variety of small cactus to create this living wreath. Cactuses are usually available in most grocery stores and large hardware stores, so making this living wreath is very accessible. Pick an array of different colors, sizes and textures or whatever cactuses are calling out to you.

11-inch wreath base
25 cactuses

PLANNING THE DESIGN

Just like the succulent wreaths, you will want to pre-plan your cactus wreath design and layout. Arrange the cactuses on a table to find a pleasing arrangement or simply start planting and adding cactuses as you move around the wreath. I like the look of clustering similar colors in areas to add some interest and to maintain balance.

PREPPING THE CACTUS

1 When working with cactuses, you will want to wear heavy garden gloves. Pick a pair that fits your hands properly. You'll want a snug fit.

2 Gently grab the base of a cactus with the forceps and pull the plant out of the plastic pot. Knock off as much of the sandy soil as possible with a screwdriver or wooden skewer. Doing this over a bucket to catch the excess soil is a good idea.

3 Give the roots a good dunk in fresh water to really clean off the root ball. As you are working with the different varieties, you'll notice some can be easily divided and used in different areas of the wreath.

PLANTING THE CACTUS

1 Be sure to take the utmost care while creating a cactus wreath. Spines will prick you at the most inopportune times. Poke holes into the wreath form with your forceps or screwdriver. Some of the cactus roots can be on the bulky side, so really open a wide hole by twisting your forceps in a circular rotation.

2 Lift each cactus with forceps and then place it in a hole. A bent piece of thick cardboard to hold or support the cactus is also a useful tool.

3 Use your forceps to push roots deep into the soil. To give some extra support while roots start, secure the plants with floral pins, but take care to not pierce the cactuses. On the outer edge of my wreath, I used a number of wire pins on the large ball cactus; gravity likes to pull them out. If you find some bare spots near the roots, add in a pinch of moss.

CARE

After planting, water weekly for one month until roots become established. Soak the wreath with a slow and gentle dribble from the hose until completely moist and then drain well. Cactuses love the heat and sun and are very drought tolerant, so this wreath will be happy outdoors. The wreath will look its best with regular watering in hotter months. Cactuses also thrive indoors with plenty of light and require very little watering.

MOSS

NATURAL MOSS

Soft velvet pillows of green moss look exquisite in wreath form. Natural moss can be gathered from the woodlands or it might be lurking in your own backyard. I collected a large bucket full from an old rain gutter on my garage. Flower shops should carry mood moss, another variety that works great for living wreath applications. Moss can look seemingly dry, brown, and lifeless until you give it a quick soak in cool fresh water. Right before your eyes, it plumps, turns green and springs to life!

15-inch round wreath form
Approximately 25 (3 x 3-inch) mosses

WRAPPING THE MOSS

1 Start with a damp wreath base.

2 There is no need to poke holes into the wreath form. Simply pack sections of moistened living moss on top of the wreath base, so moss upon moss is what we are going for. I clustered natural gathered moss and mood moss to get some color and texture variation.

3 Tie on your spool of fishing line and place on a clump of moss and gently start wrapping at 1-inch intervals to secure the moss. This is the same wrapping technique as when you wrapped the copper wire to make your wreath base. The fishing line effectively disappears into the moss.

4 Continue adding on more moss, wrapping until the entire wreath is covered.

5 Tie off the fishing line. This wreath can hang immediately after construction.

CARE OF A NATURAL MOSS WREATH

This moss wreath does best hanging in a shady location out of direct sunlight. Keep it very moist by submerging it in water for three minutes or by giving a long and gentle soak with the hose. In hotter months, you may have to moisten the wreath quite often to keep it green and plump.

IRISH <u>AND</u> SCOTCH MOSS

The dense tufts and shaggy texture of the Irish and Scotch mosses remind me of an old patchwork quilt. This wreath will be a lush carpet of emerald and chartreuse green and will bloom star-shaped white flowers in the spring and early summer. Both of these mosses are easily found at nurseries and garden centers.

11-inch square wreath form
8 Irish mosses
8 Scotch mosses

PREPPING THE MOSS

Take out the moss from its plastic pot and remove all soil, leaving just the green tuft of moss with some soil clinging to the roots. Don't be afraid to remove the bottom roots and soil. Moss thrives while planted level with the soil line.

WRAPPING THE MOSS

1 The technique for wrapping the Irish and Scotch mosses is the same as the natural moss wreath. Start with a damp wreath base. There is no need to poke holes into the wreath form. Simply pack sections of mosses on top of the wreath base, so moss upon moss is what we are going for.

2 Alternate the emerald green and chartreuse mosses, clustering like colors to create a sense of balance.

3 Tie on a spool of fishing line and place it on a clump of moss. Gently start wrapping at 1-inch intervals to secure the plant. This is the same wrapping technique as when you wrapped the copper wire to make your wreath base. The fishing line effectively disappears into the moss. Continue adding on more moss, wrapping until the entire wreath is covered.

4 Tie off the fishing line. This wreath can hang immediately after construction.

CARE OF IRISH AND SCOTCH MOSS WREATH

The Irish and Scotch moss wreath prefers a part sun and part shade location. Water the wreath thoroughly by submerging it in water for two to three minutes or by giving a long and gentle soak with water from a hose. Let the wreath dry between watering, and remember that consistency is key.

IVY

The happy variegated white-and-green leaves of ivy will perk up
any area of a garden. What a welcoming site on a front door or
garden gate!

11-inch wreath base
15 (3-inch) potted variegated ivy plants

PREPPING THE IVY PLANTS

Begin by taking the ivy plants out of the plastic pots. Using forceps, scrape off excess soil to expose the roots. Ivy plants are usually made up of smaller ivy shoots massed together, which allows for easily dividing the entire plant into smaller sections. Smaller ivy shoots are much easier to plant into your wreath than a large ivy plant.

PLANTING THE IVY

1 Start with a dampened wreath base.

2 With forceps or a screwdriver, make a hole through the moss and into the core of the wreath-base soil.

3 Grasp the base of the ivy shoot with forceps and gently place it into the hole, tucking the delicate stems inside. Plant the shoots positioned almost lying on the wreath base opposed to a more upright position. You'll want to encourage the ivy to grow around the wreath, not upwards.

4 Push the surrounding moss around the stem to secure the plant.

5 Continue planting around the entire wreath, staggering and spacing plants every 3 inches for even coverage.

6 This wreath should remain flat for two weeks before hanging.

PINNING NEW GROWTH

As the ivy plants grow and fill in, you will want to pin down the new length using some U-shaped pins. The plants will obediently put a new root down at the contact. Prune unruly leaves to keep a neat topiary-like wreath.

IVY WREATH CARE

Ivy thrives in locations out of direct sunlight and loves soil that is kept evenly moist. Water your wreath by fully submerging it for two to three minutes one to two times a week or give it a long and gentle soak with water from a garden hose.

MIXED VINE

This charming vine wreath is a combination of lush, dark emerald ivy, angel vine with its wiry stems and round foliage, and the delicate variegated white-and-green-leafed creeping fig. The refined appeal of this wreath evokes thoughts of quaint cottages with climbing vines underneath wooden eaves and along rustic garden gates.

15-inch wreath base
6 (3-inch) solid green ivy plants
6 (3-inch) angel vine plants
6 (3-inch) variegated creeping fig plants

PLANNING YOUR DESIGN

The three varieties I chose for my wreath look amazing together, each one complementing the other in different ways. However, you can just as successfully use one single type of plant for a more simplistic wreath. A solid angel vine wreath would be absolutely delightful!

PREPPING THE PLANTS

1 Carefully release the plants from their plastic pots.

2 Using forceps, scrape off excess loose soil to expose the roots. One potted ivy plant is made up of smaller ivy shoots massed together, which allows for easily dividing the entire plant into smaller sections. Smaller ivy shoots are much easier to plant into your wreath than a large ivy plant. The fig and the angel vine can't be separated like the ivy, so simply add in the entire plant.

PLANTING

1 Start with a dampened wreath base.

2 With forceps or a screwdriver, make a hole through the moss into the core of the wreath-base soil.

3 Grasp the base of the plants with forceps and gently place them into the holes, tucking the delicate stems inside. Stagger and space plants every 2 to 3 inches around the entire wreath, and be sure to add plants on the outer sides. I planted alternating with the fig, ivy, and angel vine and then repeated that same pattern for a uniform design.

4 This wreath should remain flat for two weeks before hanging.

PINNING NEW GROWTH

As the vines grow and fill in, pin down the new length using some U-shaped pins. Prune unruly leaves to keep a neat topiary-like wreath.

CARE

This mixed vine living wreath needs to be kept evenly moist and prefers filtered light, and will be happy outdoors or inside. The variegated creeping fig can be a bit of a high-maintenance specimen and will tend to develop brown crispy edges if not maintained properly. The variegated color of the small, irregular petal-shaped leaves is worth the extra care. If you choose, switch out the fig for more ivy or angel vine, or even find another vining beauty to add. Water your wreath by fully submerging it for two to three minutes one to two times a week or give it a long and gentle soak with water from a garden hose.

STRAWBERRY

Add a dash of country chic to any space with this living strawberry wreath. The leaves on the strawberry plant add wonderful texture punctuated by sweet white blossoms and tender green and red berries. Harvest the strawberries throughout summer to add to your favorite dishes, or pop them directly into your mouth. There is nothing quite like the aroma and taste of a sun-ripened strawberry freshly picked! This early summer bloomer beckons family and friends outside to enjoy a glass of strawberry lemonade on the patio.

11-inch wreath base
10 strawberry plants

PLANNING THE DESIGN

You will want to purchase young strawberry plants. This will allow for easy planting into a wreath. Any strawberry variety will work wonderfully, but be sure to pick the healthiest-looking plants.

PREPPING THE PLANTS

Gently remove the plants from their plastic pots. If plants don't slide out easily, give the side of the pot a squeeze and carefully pull out the plant. With forceps, knock off excess soil to expose the roots.

PLANTING THE STRAWBERRIES

1 Start with a dampened wreath base.

2 With forceps or a screwdriver, make a hole through the moss and into the core of the wreath-base soil.

3 Grasp the base of a strawberry plant with forceps and gently place it into the hole, tucking the stems inside.

4 Push the surrounding moss around the stems to secure the plants. Stagger and space plants 2 inches apart.

5 Strawberry plants send out long vine-like stems and leaves called runners. These can become a bit unruly and will wildly drape off your wreath. Pin down the long stems with U-shaped pins to tidy up the wreath and to keep it looking circular.

6 This wreath should lay flat for two to three weeks after planting to allow for roots to take hold before hanging.

CARE

Strawberries thrive in full sun and love moist soil. Water your wreath by fully submerging in water once or twice a week for two to three minutes or with a long and gentle soak with water from a garden hose. If you are watering by hose, spray a stream of water over the wreath, wait a few minutes and then repeat the procedure to allow the wreath to become fully saturated. Drain well before rehanging.

When the wreath fruits, the berries will need protection from sharp-eyed birds and other garden critters. One day I had luscious red berries ripening and the next day, the wreath was picked clean. Sometimes the inevitable happens, but you can help prevent garden thieves by covering your fruiting wreath with netting, or just watch the berries and pick them quickly as they ripen.

TOMATO

This summer stunner does double duty with an earthy scent and beautiful green foliage with pops of red and green. Abundant cherry tomatoes bursting with summer sunshine welcome visitors on this leafy wreath.

15-inch wreath base
18 Supersweet plants

PLANNING THE DESIGN

Look for small cherry tomato seedlings or any type of dwarf tomato plants that are bred specifically for hanging baskets. The Supersweet tomato variety I used produces small bite-sized bright red fruits. For even more color and visual punch, try mixing in an orange variety such as Sun Gold.

PREPPING THE PLANTS

Small tomato seedlings usually come in six-pack plugs. Gently squeeze the sides of the plastic container to release the small plant. Using your forceps, scrape off the excess soil to expose the delicate roots.

PLANTING THE TOMATOES

1 Start with a dampened wreath base.

2 With forceps, a wooden skewer or a screwdriver, make a hole through the moss and into the core of the wreath-base soil.

3 Twisting the forceps in a circular rotation will really open up the hole to allow for the plants to be easily slipped inside. Tuck in any loose or dangling roots with the forceps.

4 Stagger and space seedlings 3 to 4 inches apart for even coverage.

5 Once all the tomatoes are planted into the wreath, you will notice that they are all standing very tall and upright. You will think, how is this wreath going to grow and look right? Give it some time and allow for the plants to leaf out and get a little leggy. Once there is more length on the stems, that plants will naturally want to lay flat. If needed, use some U-shaped pins to hold down the stems and leaves to allow the wreath shape to be visible.

6 This wreath should remain flat for two weeks before hanging.

CARE

Keep this tomato wreath watered well and in full sun for best results. Water the wreath by fully submerging it in water two to three times a week or let the weather dictate how often. If you have trouble finding a large enough container to fully submerge the wreath, try using the lid from a large metal garbage can flipped over. Let the wreath sit in shallow water until it soaks enough water to saturate its moss/soil base, adding water if necessary. A long and gentle soak with water from a hose will also work to water any living wreath. Harvest your bounty from July through September.

HERB

A mixed herb wreath is appropriate for any home cook or garden lover. Fresh herbs are essential ingredients for cooking to add flavor to different recipes, in either sweet or savory applications. Use a mixture of your favorite herbs, or create a Herbes de Provence wreath that includes a combination of oregano, thyme, savory, marjoram, basil and rosemary. If you want to go in a more simple direction, a solid mint living wreath would be exquisite, and just think about the fragrance it would provide!

9-inch wreath base
lemon thyme
mint
thyme
basil
rosemary
chives
parsley
sage
tarragon
Remember to purchase small immature herb plants that can be easily planted into the wreath.

PLANNING THE DESIGN

Think about color and shape when selecting herbs for your wreath. What will look good together? What will provide contrast in color and texture? What herbs will you actually use and cook with? The variegated leaves of lemon thyme draping along the curving wreath base looks elegant positioned next to a dark green spiked rosemary. Cluster two basil plants in one area of the wreath and another basil plant across from the others to create balance. A single chive plant can be separated into smaller sections of bulbs and planted in different areas to give that desired spilling effect. Before you start planting, arrange the herb plants on a work surface to come up with a good design for the wreath.

PREPPING THE HERBS

Gently remove the herb plants from their plastic pots. With forceps, gently scrape off excess soil to expose the roots. If you leave too much soil clinging to the roots, you may have trouble fitting the plant into the wreath base.

PLANTING THE HERBS

1 With forceps or a screwdriver, make a hole through the moss and into the core of the wreath-base soil.

2 Grasping the base of the plant with forceps, ease it into the hole, tucking the roots inside. If you have a large tangle of roots, patiently and delicately ease the roots inside. It may take some time, but you will be able to get most of them inside. Don't be afraid if you have to remove a small portion of the roots. The plants sometimes benefit from a small trim if they're very root-bound.

3 Stagger and space herbs about 2 inches apart.

4 This wreath should remain flat for two weeks before hanging.

CARE

Herbs prefer a sunny spot with moist soil. After planting, you may need to water more frequently until the plants become more established, and ease your wreath into a full-sun location to reduce transplant shock.

Water the wreath by fully submerging it for two to three minutes one to two times a week or give it a long and gentle soak with water from a garden hose.

Harvesting and using the herbs will promote new growth and will produce a happy and healthy wreath.

LETTUCE

Make a living wreath out of heirloom lettuce and you will always have a salad at the ready! Heirloom varieties such as Rowdy Red, All Stars, Trout Back and May Queen Butterhead look stunning in wreath form. From chartreuse to speckled green and red, these lettuces will be beautiful at home atop your patio table.

Lettuce loves to grow in cooler temperatures and will do poorly in hot climates. Hot weather makes for bitter greens. This lettuce living wreath is ideal to plant in the cooler spring months and once again in the fall.

15-inch wreath base
Mixture of approximately 25 seedling plugs

PLANNING THE DESIGN

Try mixing different varieties in a random pattern or cluster similar varieties to give a more color-block appearance. Regardless of how you plant, when the lettuce grows in, you will have a wreath chock-full of tasty ruffled greens.

PREPPING THE LETTUCE

Remove the delicate lettuce plants from their plastic pots and scrape off the excess soil to expose the roots. Dip the roots in cool water to remove even more of the clinging soil.

PLANTING THE LETTUCE

1 Start with a dampened wreath base.

2 With forceps or a screwdriver, make a hole through the moss and into the core of the wreath-base soil.

3 With forceps, grasp the base of the plant and insert it into the hole, tucking in the roots. Lettuce does really well packed in close together, so spacing as close as 2 inches apart is fine.

4 Stagger the spacing so lettuce will fill in evenly.

5 This wreath should remain flat for two weeks before hanging.

HARVESTING THE LETTUCE

As the lettuce grows, clip the outer leaves first, allowing for the tight centers to keep growing and opening. The centers will eventually turn into large delicious lettuce leaves, calling out for some homemade balsamic dressing. Lettuce will mature and eventually grow a large center seed stalk. This is your signal that the lettuce leaves are bitter and your harvest is pretty much over.

CARE

Lettuce living wreaths prefer morning sun and afternoon shade, along with moist soil. To water, submerge the wreath in cool water for two to three minutes two to three times a week. You can also give the wreath a long and gentle soak with water from a garden hose. Once the lettuces have stopped producing, gently pull out the spent plants and discard. You can replant in the same holes once cooler weather has arrived.

LAVENDER

I can't imagine my garden not having lavender somewhere. I grow this scented beauty in numerous large terra cotta pots on my patio; it also peeks out from the herb garden and of course in a living wreath. Lavender is easy to grow, with the silvery tufts quite happy in their wreath home. When the rich purple heads explode with color, I'm reminded of the spectacular purple fields in France, the air heavy with scent at harvest time.

Silver foliage and aromatic purple blooms deserve a place on a sunny front door. A few heads pulled and crushed while passing by will release scented tranquility.

9-inch wreath base
8 English lavender plants
5 small French lavender seedlings

PLANNING THE DESIGN

I used English and French varieties of lavender in this lush wreath. The French variety has particularly attractive gray green notched leaves. When paired with English lavender, varying foliage colors, textures and shapes are achieved. There is also a lovely Spanish variety that blooms with curving feather-like tops. Purchasing small plants and seedlings without blooms will allow you to easily plant the lavender into a living wreath. Cluster two of the English lavender plants in four different areas of the wreath. Mix in the smaller French lavender on the outside and inside curves.

PREPPING THE LAVENDER PLANTS

Release each plant from its plastic pot and, with forceps, gently remove the soil from around the roots.

PLANTING THE LAVENDER

1 Start with a dampened wreath base.

2 With forceps or a screwdriver, make a hole through the moss and into the core of the wreath-base soil.

3 Take the lavender plants and gently fit them into the holes, using forceps to ease the root ball inside. Push down gently to secure the plant well.

4 Lay this wreath flat for two weeks before hanging.

CARE

Lavender loves sunshine and well-drained soil. Newly planted lavender can become quite thirsty, so make sure your wreath is getting plenty of water until the roots become established. One to two times a week, fully submerge the wreath in water for two to three minutes or give it a long and gentle soak of water from a garden hose.

SPIDER PLANT

The slender leaves of the striped green-and-white spider plant lovingly embrace the curved wreath base. As the larger "mother" spider plants continue to grow, they will shoot off smaller "baby" plants, also known as plantlets. You can clip this new growth and plant it into another living wreath!

Spider plants are hardy, easy-to-care-for plants and grow happily in a variety of climates. They have also proven to be very effective with clearing indoor air pollutants.

9-inch wreath base
7 (3-inch) spider plants

PREPPING THE PLANTS

Gently remove the plants from their plastic pots. Using forceps, scrape off the excess soil to expose the roots. Spider plants have water-rich tuberous-looking roots that can be on the bulky side, but each plant can be divided into small more manageable plugs. Some of the roots may break off. Don't worry, though! This will not harm the plant, and new roots will grow rather quickly.

PLANTING

1 Start with a dampened wreath base.

2 With forceps or a screwdriver, make a hole through the moss and into the core of the wreath-base soil.

3 Stagger and space plants every 2 inches, evenly covering the entire wreath.

4 Grasp the base of each plant with forceps and gently place it into a hole, tucking the stems inside. During planting is when you will most likely break off some of the tuberous roots. The plant will adapt just fine; however, make sure to get the bulk of the roots planted inside the wreath.

5 Use some U-shaped pins to secure around the roots if added support is needed or to hold down flyaway longer leaves.

6 This wreath should lay flat for two weeks before hanging.

CARE

Bouffant spider plants add texture and beauty to an interior room where light is sufficient. A spider plant wreath will thrive in a warm location in a house out of direct sunlight; harsh sun exposure can scorch the tender leaves. On the other hand, if the wreath is not getting enough sun, the variegated stripe pattern and color will fade. For best results, hang the wreath near a window that receives plenty of indirect light. Frequent misting will give the humidity spider plants love. If any browning occurs on the tips of the leaves, simply give them a trim with sharp scissors. Allow soil and moss to dry slightly before watering. Fully submerge the wreath in water once a week or place it in a sink and give it a gentle soak with water from the faucet. Drain the wreath well before rehanging.

BEGONIA AND JADE

The lush and glossy bronze patina of wax begonias is paired with green rosette-like leaves of strawberry begonias that hide a blushing pink underside and plump green leaves of jade. Together they are shown off to perfection in a living wreath. Wax begonias provide brilliant blooms, the strawberry begonias deliver texture and jade lends a natural relaxed look.

Strawberry begonias send out numerous thin runners that will produce small plantlets (similar to strawberry plants). You can clip the new growth and propagate into another living wreath.

This begonia and jade wreath can make a home outside, but it will also flourish indoors with bright light. Outside or in, this wreath will breathe life into any space.

9-inch wreath base
12 small begonias
5 (3-inch) strawberry begonias
6 jade cuttings

PREPPING THE PLANTS

Treat the jade as you would other succulents, taking cuttings and allowing them to callus over for two days prior to planting. One medium jade plant should yield six to eight jade cuttings.

The wax begonias were leafed without any blooms, which allows for easy planting into a wreath. Gently remove the begonia plants from their plastic pots. Using forceps, scrape off the excess soil to expose the roots.

PLANTING

1   Start with a dampened wreath base.

2   With forceps or a screwdriver, make a hole through the moss and into the core of the wreath-base soil.

3   Grasp the base of the plants with the forceps and carefully slip it inside, tucking in the roots.

4   Stagger and space begonias every 2 to 3 inches around the wreath, clustering jade cuttings around the begonias.

5   Use some U-shaped pins to secure jade cuttings until the roots take hold.

6   This wreath should lay flat after planting for five to six weeks, allowing roots to take form before hanging.

CARE

This begonia and jade living wreath will thrive outdoors in a partial sun location. Too much direct sunlight may burn the begonia leaves. To water, fully submerge the wreath once or twice a week for two to three minutes or give it a long and gentle soak with water from a garden hose. The soil within this wreath likes to remain moist. Keep the wreath flat for five to six weeks, until the jade cuttings have taken root.

BRONZE CLOVER
AND GROUND COVER

Get these ground creepers out from underfoot to where they can really shine! Pairing complementary colors make this unique wreath a showstopper. Chocolate ball sedum and bronze clover come to life when paired with the delicate trailing stems of chartreuse creeping jenny.

15-inch wreath base
3 creeping jenny
2 sedum
3 bronze clovers

PLANNING THE DESIGN

I love the look of clustering brightly colored foliage within a living wreath, to allow other darker plants to really pop. I grouped the creeping jenny together in two different areas of the wreath and clustered in the sedum and clover to achieve a sense of balance. Before planting, lay out your design on a tabletop.

PREPPING THE PLANTS

Gently remove the plants from their plastic pots. Using forceps, scrape off excess soil to expose the roots. The bronze clover has fairly shallow roots and can be easily divided into smaller sections.

PLANTING

1 Start with a dampened wreath base.

2 With forceps or a screwdriver, make a hole through the moss and into the core of the wreath-base soil.

3 Grasp the base of the plants with forceps and carefully slip it inside, tucking in the roots.

4 Stagger and space plants every 3 inches around the wreath. Creeping jenny is a vining beauty and will need to be secured using U-shaped pins to keep it looking orderly.

5 This wreath should lay flat for two weeks before hanging.

CARE

This living wreath will be at its happiest in a partial sun location. Keep it moist until the roots become established. Fully submerge the wreath in water one to two times a week for two to three minutes or give it a long and gentle soak of water from a garden hose.

In warmer climates, this wreath will require a little more shade. In cooler climates, it will need more sun. It's also fun to note that the bronze clover will become redder in the sun and greener in the shade.

LEAFY
HOUSEPLANT

It's the dead of winter and you need something alive and green in the house to give you hope for spring's arrival. The garden centers are bare and you need to get your hands on some plants *pronto*! Check the houseplant section of local grocery stores and you'll most likely find a nice array of leafy houseplants. Pick eight to ten 3-inch plants and make an inexpensive and accessible wreath anytime of year. I keep my leafy ring on a coffee table atop a pottery plate to keep the table protected from any moisture. It's thriving and adds a living touch that each room deserves.

The following plants inspired me to create this leafy houseplant living wreath.

9-inch wreath base

3 Polka-dot plants: Beautiful marbled green, white and pink leaves

2 aluminum plants: Dark green foliage looks as if it has been brushed with metallic silver paint

2 pileas (pronounced /py-lee-uh/): Thick leaves with a burgundy-coppery sheen have depressed veins, giving a quilted appearance

2 strawberry begonias: Green rosette-like leaves show a blushing pink underside

PLANNING THE DESIGN

If you can't find the exact varieties listed above, there are sure to be other wonderful small houseplant varieties available. Always purchase small healthy-looking plants that will thrive in the same environment, from soil to light conditions.

PREPPING THE PLANTS

Gently remove the plants from their plastic pots. Using forceps, scrape off excess soil to expose the roots.

PLANTING

1   Start with a dampened wreath base.

2   With forceps or a screwdriver, make a hole through the moss and into the core of the wreath-base soil.

3   Grasp the base of the plant with forceps and gently slide the root ball inside. Tuck in any loose roots, and push the surrounding moss down around the base of the plant to secure.

4   Cluster the pilea plants together and then mix the other varieties all the way around the wreath, remembering to keep a sense of balance. Stagger and space plants every 3 inches.

5   Lay this wreath flat for two weeks before hanging to allow the roots to take hold.

CARE

This leafy houseplant living wreath will do best in a medium filtered light location. Too much sun will damage the lush and tender foliage. Keep the wreath consistently moist by fully submerging it in water for two to three minutes once or twice a week. You can also give the wreath a long and gentle soak in a kitchen sink. Trim any browning leaves and pinch back new growth to keep the wreath more manicured. Houseplants prefer a monthly mild liquid fertilizer to keep them looking their best.